HomeBuilders *Couples Series*®

mastering
Money
in Your Marriage

By Ron Blue

*"Unless the Lord
builds the house,
its builders
labor in vain"*
(Psalm 127:1a).

FAMILYLIFE™
Bringing Timeless Principles Home
Little Rock, Arkansas

Group
Loveland, Colorado

Group's R.E.A.L. Guarantee® to you:

This Group resource incorporates our R.E.A.L. approach to ministry—one that encourages long-term retention and life transformation. It's ministry that's:

Relational
Because learner-to-learner interaction enhances learning and builds Christian friendships.

Experiential
Because what learners experience through discussion and action sticks with them up to 9 times longer than what they simply hear or read.

Applicable
Because the aim of Christian education is to equip learners to be both hearers and doers of God's Word.

Learner-based
Because learners understand and retain more when the learning process takes into consideration how they learn best.

Visit our Web site: **www.group.com**

Credits
FamilyLife
Editor: David Boehi
Assistant Editor: Julie Denker

Group Publishing, Inc.
Editor: Matt Lockhart
Creative Development Editor: Paul Woods
Chief Creative Officer: Joani Schultz
Copy Editor: Deirdre Brouer
Art Director: Jenette L. McEntire
Cover Art Director: Jeff A. Storm
Computer Graphic Artist: Anita M. Cook
Cover Photographer: FPG International
Illustrator: Ken Jacobsen
Production Manager: Peggy Naylor

ISBN 0-7644-2241-3
20 19 18 17 16 15 14 13 12   15 14 13 12 11 10 09 08 07 06

Printed in the United States of America.

How to Let the Lord Build Your House
and not labor in vain

●

The HomeBuilders Couples Series®: A small-group Bible study dedicated to making your family all that God intended.

FamilyLife is a division of Campus Crusade for Christ International, an evangelical Christian organization founded in 1951 by Bill Bright. FamilyLife was started in 1976 to help fulfill the Great Commission by strengthening marriages and families and then equipping them to go to the world with the gospel of Jesus Christ. The FamilyLife Marriage Conference is held in most major cities throughout the United States and is one of the fastest-growing marriage conferences in America today. "FamilyLife Today," a daily radio program hosted by Dennis Rainey, is heard on hundreds of stations across the country. Information on all resources offered by FamilyLife may be obtained by contacting us at the address, telephone number, or World Wide Web site listed below.

Dennis Rainey, Executive Director
FamilyLife
P.O. Box 8220
Little Rock, AR 72221-8220
1-800-FL-TODAY
www.familylife.com

A division of Campus Crusade for Christ International
Bill Bright, Founder and President

About the Sessions

Each session in this study is composed of the following categories: Warm-Up, Blueprints, Wrap-Up, and HomeBuilders Project. A description of each of these categories follows:

Warm-Up (15 minutes)

 The purpose of Warm-Up is to help people unwind from a busy day and get to know each other better. Typically the first point in Warm-Up is an exercise that is meant to be fun while introducing the topic of the session. The ability to share in fun with others is important in building relationships. Another component of Warm-Up is the Project Report (except in Session One), which is designed to provide accountability for the HomeBuilders Project that is to be completed by couples between sessions.

Blueprints (60 minutes)

 This is the heart of the study. In this part of each session, people answer questions related to the topic of study and look to God's Word for understanding. Some of the questions are to be answered by couples, in subgroups, or in the group at large. There are notes in the margin or instructions within a question that designate these groupings.

Wrap-Up (15 minutes)

This category serves to "bring home the point" and wind down a session in an appropriate fashion.

HomeBuilders Project (60 minutes)

This project is the unique application step in a HomeBuilders study. Before leaving a meeting, couples are encouraged to "Make a Date" to do this project prior to the next meeting. Most HomeBuilders Projects contain three sections: (1) As a Couple—a brief exercise designed to get the date started in a fun way; (2) Individually—a section of questions for husbands and wives to answer separately; and (3) Interact as a Couple— an opportunity for couples to share their answers with each other and to make application in their lives.

In addition to the above regular features, occasional activities are labeled "For Extra Impact." These are activities that generally provide a more active or visual way to make a particular point. Be mindful that people within a group have different learning styles. While most of what is presented is verbal, a visual or active exercise now and then helps engage more of the senses and appeals to people who learn best by seeing, touching, and doing.

About the Author

After graduating from Indiana University with a master's degree in business administration, Ron Blue joined the management firm of Peat, Marwick, Mitchell & Co.

In 1970 Ron founded an Indianapolis-based CPA firm that has grown to be one of the fifty largest CPA firms in the United States. After leaving the CPA firm in 1977, Ron became administrative vice president of Leadership Dynamics International.

Convinced that Christians would better handle their personal finances if they were counseled objectively with the highest technical expertise and from a biblical perspective, he founded Ronald Blue & Co., a fee-only financial planning firm, in 1979. With offices throughout the U.S., RBC offers financial, estate, and investment counsel to individuals and organizations.

Ron is the author of nine books on personal finance from a biblical perspective, including the best seller *Master Your Money*, first published in 1986 and now in its twenty-seventh printing. He is featured in the popular, six-part *Master Your Money* video series, produced by Walk Thru the Bible Ministries, and used in over 5,500 churches.

Most recently Ron has written *Money Talks and So Can We* and *Generous Living*, both published by Zondervan. In addition, he has co-authored *Raising Money-Smart Kids* and *A Woman's Guide to Financial Peace of Mind* with his wife, Judy.

Ron has appeared on numerous radio and television programs, including *Focus on the Family, Family News in Focus, The 700 Club, Prime Time America,* and *Moody Radio Open Line.* He is a regular contributor to several national Christian magazines.

Ron and Judy live in Atlanta. They have five children and four grandchildren.

Contents

Acknowledgments

There are many to whom I am deeply indebted for encouragement, assistance, and critical evaluation in the production of this Bible study. When Dennis Rainey approached me with the prospect of preparing this study, he saw something in what I had done that I did not see. He was confident that the materials I had developed in ministering to others could be used in a much more significant way and minister to far greater numbers of people. I am thankful to Dennis and his wife, Barbara, for modeling many things, but most of all, for modeling a God-honoring marriage and family.

Dave Boehi has been a very sensitive, gentle, but effective editor through this process. He has encouraged me through many revisions without being critical in any way. He has been extremely encouraging, and I sincerely appreciate the time spent working with him.

I am also very appreciative of Julie Denker's work from the beginning of the project. What she did in editing and in coordinating the field test was largely unseen but very valuable and meaningful to me.

Most importantly I would like to thank my wife, Judy, for living out the principles taught in this study and for teaching me by example, my children who have been patient and helpful throughout the writing process, and my staff as they suffered through changes in schedule that never seemed to end.

Last of all, I appreciate the comments and constructive criticism that came from the test groups who have contributed a great deal to making this study what it is.

Foreword

When the time came to select an author for the subject of finances in the HomeBuilders Couples Series, several fine names came to mind. And after careful consideration, we determined that there is nobody more qualified to design a practical, small-group Bible study for you than Ron Blue.

Not only is Ron a best-selling author, a Christian leader, a director of a large organization, and a board member of some excellent Christian organizations, but he is also a dedicated family man. Ron and his wife, Judy, are committed to helping their five children and others to manage their money well.

Wrapped in the pages of this study are challenging questions that will lead you and your spouse to evaluate the kind of stewards you are of the resources God has entrusted to you. It will spark contemplation and ignite the interaction that you need to bring about change in how you handle your finances.

Ron delivers what you and I need in a culture of tremendous pressure and change. You will have the opportunity to interact with your spouse and with other couples in this study. Then, at the end of each session, you'll find some "blue-chip" projects that will enable you to change the convictions you develop from this study into practical application and day-to-day living.

This study is solidly biblical and simply practical. You will find, as my wife, Barbara, and I have, that Ron Blue will equip you and your spouse to work through financial difficulties and to develop a sound financial plan.

Dennis Rainey

Executive Director, FamilyLife

Introduction

When a man and woman are married, they stand before a room of witnesses and proclaim their commitment to a lifetime of love. They recite a sacred vow "to have and to hold...from this day forward...to love, honor, and cherish...for better, for worse...for richer, for poorer...in sickness and in health...as long as we both shall live."

It's a happy day, perhaps the happiest in their lives. And yet, once the honeymoon ends, once the emotions of courtship and engagement subside, many couples realize that "falling in love" and building a good marriage are two different things. Keeping those vows is much more difficult than they thought it would be.

Otherwise intelligent people, who would not think of buying a car, investing money, or even going to the grocery store without some initial planning, enter into marriage with no plan of how to make that relationship succeed.

But God has already provided the plan, a set of blueprints for building a truly God-honoring marriage. His plan is designed to enable a man and woman to grow together in a mutually satisfying relationship and then to reach out to others with the love of Christ. Ignoring this plan leads only to isolation and separation between husband and wife. It's a pattern evident in so many homes today: Failure to follow God's blueprints results in wasted effort, bitter disappointment, and, in far too many cases, divorce.

In response to this need in marriages today, FamilyLife has developed a series of small-group studies called the HomeBuilders Couples Series.

You could complete this study alone with your spouse, but we strongly urge you to either form or join a group of couples studying this material. You will find that the questions in each session not only help you grow closer to your spouse, but they help create a special environment of warmth and fellowship as you study together how to build the type of marriage you desire. Participating in a HomeBuilders group could be one of the highlights of your married life.

The Bible: Your Blueprints for a God-Honoring Marriage

You will notice as you proceed through this study that the Bible is used frequently as the final authority on issues of life and marriage. Although written thousands of years ago, this Book still speaks clearly and powerfully about the conflicts and struggles faced by men and women. The Bible is God's Word— his blueprints for building a God-honoring home and for dealing with the practical issues of living.

We encourage you to have a Bible with you for each session. For this series we use the New International Version as our primary reference. Another excellent translation is the New American Standard Bible.

Ground Rules

Each group session is designed to be enjoyable and informative—and nonthreatening. Three simple ground rules will help ensure that everyone feels comfortable and gets the most out of the experience:

1. Don't share anything that would embarrass your spouse.

2. You may pass on any question you don't want to answer.

3. If possible, plan to complete the HomeBuilders Project as a couple between group sessions.

A Few Quick Notes About Leading a HomeBuilders Group

1. Leading a group is much easier than you may think! A group leader in a HomeBuilders session is really a "facilitator." As a leader, your goal is simply to guide the group through the discussion questions. You don't need to teach the material—in fact, we don't want you to! The special dynamic of a HomeBuilders group is that couples teach themselves.

2. This material is designed to be used in a home study, but it also can be adapted for use in a Sunday school environment. (See page 113 for more information about this option.)

3. We have included a section of Leader's Notes in the back of this book. Be sure to read through these notes before leading a session; they will help you prepare.

4. For more material on leading a HomeBuilders group, get a copy of the *HomeBuilders Leader Guide*, by Drew and Kit Coons. This book is an excellent resource that provides helpful guidelines on how to start a study, how to keep discussion moving, and much more.

A Word About Finances

Did you know that the Bible contains more than two thousand verses dealing with money and money management? In my opinion, this reflects God's understanding of human nature, and how we handle our money reveals much about our character and spiritual commitment.

Any married couple will attest to the fact that many of their conflicts and disagreements revolve around their finances. So this study has two primary objectives in mind for you: (1) to help you identify and grapple with some of the biblical principles and issues regarding the whole concept of wealth and money management, and (2) to provide you with some practical guidance for handling your own personal finances.

You'll find that *Mastering Money in Your Marriage* is as much a financial workbook as it is a small-group Bible study. The exercises you'll go through are crucial if you want to be serious about handling your money wisely. Many people hear these biblical principles but don't act on them; my prayer is that you'll take the time to apply what you'll learn.

Ron Blue

Putting Money in Its Place

Managing money wisely is a challenge for any couple, regardless of income level.

W A R M • U P   15   M I N U T E S

By the Numbers

As a fun way of getting to know everyone in the group better, work together to calculate the grand total within this group for each of the following items:

- number of years married
- number of kids living at home
- number of household moves since wedding
- current number of pets
- approximate number of miles from home to this group's meeting place

Getting Connected

Pass your book around the room, and have couples write their names, phone numbers, and e-mail addresses.

NAME, PHONE, & E-MAIL

NAME, PHONE, & E-MAIL

NAME, PHONE, & E-MAIL

NAME, PHONE, & E-MAIL

NAME, PHONE, & E-MAIL

NAME, PHONE, & E-MAIL

NAME, PHONE, & E-MAIL

For Extra Impact

Numbers Game: This exercise is a fun way to introduce the issues of managing money.

Try the following exercise. When the leader says, "go," you will have thirty seconds to find the number one, circle it, find the number two, circle it, and so on, until you have circled all ninety numbers. Do not start until the leader says, "go." You must find the numbers in sequence.

```
1           61          13          42          74          14
    41          9               70
        45          81          18          22      46
17          21                  86
        89          49              34      2       30
    37   5      69          38              50
        85              78      6           10
            29              90
25              65          82          26          58
        33              54          62
    53      57          66
        73      77
    15      79  39          32          76      16
31              71
        3       55          80          8       40
                    28      24      56
47      83          72          52
            27                          4
    7           67          12
        51      11              88
75                                  60
                        36      20
    19      23      43          48
        87              44
35          59  63      68      84      64
```

After thirty seconds are up, discuss the following questions:

- What feelings did you experience as you looked for numbers?

- What is the key to completing this task quickly?

- How is this exercise similar to the challenge of managing money wisely?

We live in a world that worships money but doesn't know how to use it wisely. The world says, "Spend! Spend! Spend!" Unfortunately, it also says, "Borrow! Borrow! Borrow!" As a result, many people find it all too easy to get into financial trouble.

The Need for a Plan

If you have a large group, form smaller groups of about six people to answer the Blueprints questions. Unless otherwise noted, answer the questions in your subgroup. After finishing each section, take time for subgroups to share their answers with the whole group.

1. What are some common financial questions and struggles couples face today?

2. How do you think most couples deal with the financial pressures they face?

3. What additional concerns might a Christian couple have?

4. Materially speaking, how do you think a Christian ought to live in our culture?

5. What are some of the issues couples face in making sound financial decisions?

Financial Needs and Priorities

6. What are your biggest financial concerns right now?

Answer questions 6 and 7 with your spouse. After answering, you may want to share an appropriate insight or discovery with the group.

7. What do you believe your top two highest financial priorities should be?

The Role of Money

8. Read the following scenario:
Congratulations! You're a farmer—a *very* successful farmer—and you have just brought in a record crop of wheat. In fact, this year's harvest is the kind that farmers dream about. Not only was the harvest plentiful, the market is at an all-time high for wheat. You are in the enviable position of being financially secure for years.

- Now that you've had a successful harvest, how do you plan to allocate this windfall of resources?

9. Read the parable of the rich fool in Luke 12:16-21, then answer these questions:

- How do you think the rich man saw himself?

• Why do you think God called him a fool? Where did the rich man go wrong?

• In what ways was your response to question 8 similar to the plans of the rich man in this parable?

10. Read Luke 12:15. What principles from this verse are important to keep in mind as you try to manage money wisely? Why?

11. Now read Luke 12:22-31. According to this passage, what is the key to the "things" we need? How is this accomplished?

HomeBuilders Principle:
Wealth will never satisfy a person's basic needs for security and significance—only God can.

W R A P • U P   15   M I N U T E S

Leader: After doing the Wrap-Up activity, close this session with prayer, and encourage couples to Make a Date for this session's HomeBuilders Project before they leave.

When it comes to money and marriage it is important to have a basic understanding of what your spouse's attitude and values toward finances are. By knowing your similarities and differences, you can work better as a team in attempting to master money.

Consider the following categories. Where would you place your spouse? Where do you think your spouse would place you? On the spectrum lines, place a Y where you see yourself and an S where you see your spouse. Then pair up with your spouse and compare results!

DINING OUT

Fast food _____ Gourmet meal

GIFT GIVING

Generous and _____ Practical
extravagant   and thrifty

SHOPPING HABITS

Discount center _____ Designer
                                                 boutique

MONEY MANAGEMENT

Saver _____ Spender

CHECKBOOK

Always knows _____ Knows when
the exact balance   he or she is
                                               out of checks

CREDIT CARDS

Plastic pal _____ Evil enemy

After comparing answers with your spouse, answer
these questions as a group. (Remember, don't share
anything that would embarrass your spouse.)

- In which category are you and your spouse most
  alike? different?

- How can being aware of your differences be
  helpful as you try and manage money wisely in
  your marriage?

Make a Date

Make a date with your spouse to meet before the next session to complete the HomeBuilders Project. At the next session, your leader will ask you to share one aspect of this experience.

DATE

TIME

LOCATION

HOMEBUILDERS PROJECT   6 0   M I N U T E S

As a Couple [10 minutes]

Share about some of your early experiences with money by answering the following questions:
- When do you remember first receiving an allowance? How much did you receive? What did you do with it?

- What is something you worked and saved for when you were a teenager?

- What is one lesson about money you have learned that has really stuck with you?

Individually [20 minutes]

1. What is the most important insight you have gained from this session?

2. What are some good things (areas of confidence) about your personal finances?

3. What are some not-so-good things (areas of concern) about your finances?

4. What would you say is the number one financial need in your marriage right now? Explain.

5. A key factor in managing your money wisely in your marriage is the level of unity between you and your spouse on financial goals, priorities, and values. On a scale of one (low) to ten (high), how would you rate the level of unity between you and your spouse on financial matters?

6. What are one or two specific steps you could take to create more unity with your spouse?

7. Pray that God would strengthen the spirit of unity in your marriage and that this course would help equip you to better master money in your marriage.

Interact as a Couple [30 minutes]

1. Share your answers to the questions you both answered individually. *Note:* Resolve that you will not argue! Be open, kind, and understanding as you address sensitive issues.

2. Read the following personal pledge with your spouse:

"I pledge to you that I will use the next five sessions of this HomeBuilders study to build, strengthen, and encourage our marriage. I will make this study a priority in my schedule by faithfully keeping our dates, working through the projects, and participating in the group discussions."

_____

(signature)

Will you honor your spouse by making this pledge your special commitment to him or her? If so, sign this pledge in your spouse's book.

3. Close in prayer. Thank God for providing for you in the past. Pray for financial wisdom for now and the future.

Remember to bring your calendar to the next session to Make a Date.

Stewardship

Stewardship is managing God's resources
to accomplish God-given goals.

W A R M • U P   15   M I N U T E S

"Can I Borrow Your Car?"

You have loaned your brand-new car to your friend Bill.
When Bill returns the car, it has a crumpled fender, broken headlight, and missing bumper. When Bill hands
you the keys, he apologizes for the damage and asks if
you would mind loaning him the car again next week.

- What would you say to Bill?
- Why do we expect our friends to treat our property
  differently than Bill did?
- When has something like this happened to you?
- How is this situation similar to how we care for
  what God gives us?

Project Report

Share one thing you learned from last session's Home-Builders Project.

BLUEPRINTS   60 MINUTES

In this session we are going to explore how our stewardship of God's property is an important measure of our faithfulness to God.

Attitudes About Money

If you have a large group, form smaller groups of about six people to answer the Blueprints questions. Unless otherwise noted, answer the questions in your subgroup. After finishing each section, take time for subgroups to share their answers with the whole group.

1. What guidelines do you think most people use in managing their money?

2. In what ways do you think a Christian's attitude toward money should be different from that of a non-Christian?

3. How has your attitude toward money changed over time? What caused you to change your attitude?

4. Read Psalm 24:1-2 and Colossians 1:16. What do these verses say to you about your possessions?

HomeBuilders Principle:
God owns it all.

Examples of Stewardship

Webster's New World College Dictionary defines a steward as "one who acts as a supervisor or administrator, as of finances and property, for another or others."

Read Matthew 25:14-30.

5. What were the responsibilities of the servants in this parable?

6. Compare and contrast the servants in this parable. What characteristics distinguish them from each other?

7. What do you think would have happened if the lazy servant had ventured and lost the talent instead of putting it in the ground? Why?

8. What can you learn from this parable about your own stewardship responsibilities?

HomeBuilders Principle:
Stewardship means using the resources God has entrusted to you to accomplish his plans and purposes.

Challenges of Stewardship

9. Read Luke 16:10-12. What are the standards for a steward in these verses?

10. Read Luke 16:13. Why is it that people "cannot serve both God and Money"? Have you found this to be true in your life? If so, how?

11. When have you felt like the resources God has entrusted to you (money, possessions, time, and talents) were used in a particularly God-honoring way?

Answer questions 11 and 12 with your spouse. After answering, you may want to share an appropriate insight or discovery with the group.

12. How has God used money to help you grow in your faith?

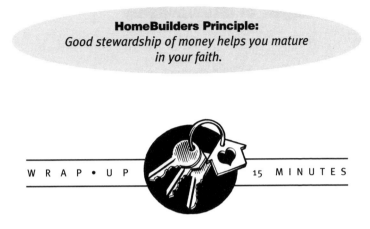

HomeBuilders Principle:
Good stewardship of money helps you mature in your faith.

W R A P • U P   15 M I N U T E S

Leader: For this exercise, assign a different asset to each team. See note 5 on page 123 in the Leader's Notes.

Consider yourself an employee of the Kingdom Corporation. The owner, a very powerful and wealthy individual, has to travel for business to a remote area and will be gone for the next two years. You and your associates have been left in charge of managing various company assets.

Form three teams. Your team will be assigned one of three assets to manage: (1) $1 million, (2) the facility (a 100,000 square-foot multiuse facility), (3) the auto fleet (a dozen brand-new minivans).

Spend five to ten minutes with your team to develop a resource-management plan. Decide how you are going to manage your assigned resource, and devise a strategy. Then present your plan, including the thinking behind your strategy, to the other teams.

After each team has presented, discuss the following questions:

- Regardless of your team's asset, what was your team's goal? Why?

- Which trait do you think is more important to the owner: action or results? Explain.

- How does this activity relate to the way we handle the resources God has given us?

- What role does faith play in stewardship?

Make a Date

Make a date with your spouse to meet before the next session to complete the HomeBuilders Project. At the next session, your leader will ask you to share one aspect of this experience.

DATE

TIME

LOCATION

As a Couple [5 minutes]

Talk about a financial blunder from your past that you can laugh about now.

- What is one of the worst financial decisions you've ever made?
- What did you learn from this?

Individually [20 minutes]

1. What is one way you have been challenged in this session to be a better steward? What are you going to do about this?

2. Think of a recent frustration you've had regarding money. What might God be trying to teach you?

3. Make a list of the three material possessions you would most hate to lose:

-

-

-

How can you exercise good stewardship of these possessions?

4. Consider the following three resources:

Money

Possessions

Time

- Which of these resources is easiest for you to manage with good stewardship? Why?

- Which resource is the most difficult? Why?

- What is one example that illustrates God-honoring stewardship of each resource?

5. In what ways do you struggle with acknowledging God's total ownership of all your resources?

Interact as a Couple [35 minutes]

1. Discuss your answers to the previous questions.

2. Beyond finances and possessions is a very valuable resource that you have been entrusted with: time. It is not unusual to hear someone complain about not having enough time. Like money, time can be spent or wasted. But unlike money, lost time cannot be replaced.

Spend some time talking about a season in life when you hope to have more time.

- Dream together by focusing on how you would like to spend your time. What would you like to invest yourself in?

• Challenge yourself with this question: Does this demonstrate good stewardship?

3. Create a sentence together about your roles as stewards. Write this statement on a sticky note or index card, and place it where it will remind you to manage God's resources in a way that honors him.

4. In prayer, acknowledge that everything you have belongs to the true Owner—God, who owns it all—and accept your stewardship responsibility.

Remember to bring your calendar to the next session to Make a Date. Plan to bring your checkbook as well.

Financial Priorities

Every financial decision you make is ultimately
a spiritual decision about how God would like
you to prioritize your money.

W A R M • U P   15   M I N U T E S

"Thank You, Aunt Harriet!"

You have just been notified that your great-aunt Harriet
passed away at the age of one hundred. Her will desig-
nates fifty thousand dollars in cash for you. There's only
one condition: It all must be spent within thirty days.

Individually, make a list of how you would use the money.

Item	Estimated Cost

Total: $50,000

After everyone has given an account of his or her funds, discuss these questions:

- What did you consider as you decided how to use the money?
- Think of an item that you initially thought about adding to your list but ultimately decided against. Why did you decide against that item?

Project Report
Share one thing you learned from last session's Home-Builders Project.

BLUEPRINTS   60 MINUTES

Influences on Financial Priorities

If you have a large group, form smaller groups of about six people to answer the Blueprints questions. Unless otherwise noted, answer the questions in your subgroup. After finishing each section, take time for subgroups to share their answers with the whole group.

1. What are some ways your financial priorities are influenced by our society? How much pressure do you feel to keep up with those around you?

2. How does your relationship with God influence your financial priorities?

3. Rank the following priorities from one to five in order of the influence they have on your financial decisions:

_____family

_____friends

_____neighbors

_____God

_____culture

Which priority did you rank the highest and why?

4. What is one nonfinancial priority you have (such as completing a task, or achieving a personal goal)? In what way can money help you accomplish this?

HomeBuilders Principle:
Money is not an end in itself; it's a tool that can help you meet God-honoring priorities.

Examining Financial Priorities

It is good to keep in mind that disagreements over financial decisions are inevitable in marriage because any two people will, at times, have different priorities for spending money.

Answer questions 5 through 7 with your spouse. After answering, you may want to share an appropriate insight or discovery with the group.

5. Looking at your checkbook, review the checks you've written over the last month. (If you don't have your checkbook with you, think about the checks you've written over the last month.) What conclusions might someone else make from this evidence about your financial priorities?

6. As a couple, how do you generally decide what your financial priorities should be?

7. What do you agree are financial priorities? What do you tend to value differently?

8. After each couple has chosen one of the following passages, read your passage with your spouse and discuss what wisdom, guidance, or principle it offers us as we think of setting financial priorities. Then read your passage to the group, and share any insights you may have gained.

It's OK for a couple to choose more than one passage or for more than one couple to choose the same passage depending on the number of couples in the group.

- Isaiah 55:2
- Matthew 6:33
- Luke 14:28
- John 6:27
- James 4:13-15

9. Read Mark 10:17-23. What problem did this man have with his financial priorities? How can sometimes having *too* much create problems?

Biblical Priorities for Money Management

Couples can avoid conflicts over financial decisions by agreeing on their priorities as a couple and recognizing their legitimate differences and the need to compromise. Examining biblical priorities for money management can aid a couple in developing mutual financial priorities.

10. The Bible includes over two thousand verses about money and money management. The following verses provide instructions for five financial priorities. After each couple has chosen one of the following passages, read and discuss it with your spouse. Then read your passage to the group, and explain how it relates to money management.

- Psalm 37:21
- Proverbs 3:9
- Proverbs 31:16
- Romans 13:6-7
- 1 Timothy 5:8

Biblical Priorities and the Financial Planning Process

The following diagram of the financial planning process shows the crucial role biblical priorities play in financial planning. When you determine your financial situation by appropriately dividing your income among the five financial priorities the Bible specifies, you'll begin developing the ability to meet the long-range objectives that are shown. Money allocated to one of the five priority-spending areas will affect your ability to spend in the other four areas.

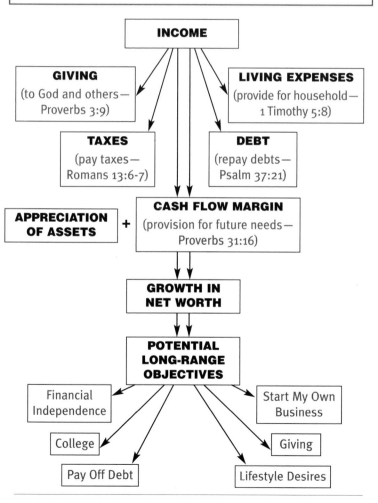

11. Which category do you find easiest to make a priority? the most difficult?

12. What do you need to do to better organize your finances around biblical priorities?

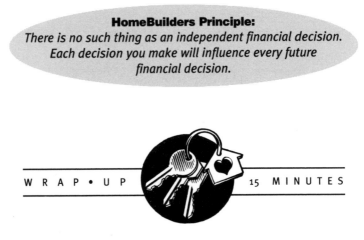

HomeBuilders Principle:
There is no such thing as an independent financial decision. Each decision you make will influence every future financial decision.

W R A P • U P   15   M I N U T E S

Look again at the list you made in the Warm-Up section. This time see how quickly you can agree on a list with your spouse. There must be 100 percent agreement and at least three items on the list.

Item	Estimated Cost
1.	
2.	
3.	
	Total: $50,000

After making your list, share it with the group. After every couple has shared its list, discuss these questions:

- How easy was it for you to reach a consensus with your spouse?

- How did you compromise when you didn't agree with each other on an item?

- How was this decision process like or unlike the financial decisions you make on a regular basis?

Make a Date

Make a date with your spouse to meet before the next session to complete the HomeBuilders Project. At the next session, your leader will ask you to share one aspect of this experience.

DATE

TIME

LOCATION

HOMEBUILDERS PROJECT   6 0   M I N U T E S

Interact as a Couple [60 minutes]
This session's HomeBuilders Project will require you and your spouse to work together to analyze how you allocated your money over the last complete month.

Understanding how you are now spending money is the first step toward gaining control of your finances. By completing the following Expense Summary, you will gain a better understanding of what your financial priorities have been. (People are often surprised when they compare their actual financial priorities to what they have believed them to be.) You'll also be able to start making decisions about how to change your spending habits. This exercise will begin to give you tremendous freedom in your financial life as you take control of your spending.

When filling out the Expense Summary, use exact numbers as much as possible. You will want to have your checking account and credit card statements handy. Don't forget to account for expenses you incur monthly but pay for bimonthly, quarterly, semiannually, or annually. You will also want to refer to the Expense Category Descriptions on page 53, which give detailed examples of typical expenses for each expense category.

In addition to the Expense Summary on the next page, there is an expanded version of this chart in the Appendix (p. 139). This version is for couples who are interested in breaking out their expenses in greater detail.

Expense Summary

(For: _____/_____**)**
    month,   year

Net Income (after taxes): $ _____

Expense Category	Amount Paid Last Month	Usual Monthly Cost
Charitable giving	$ _____	$ _____
Debt payments	_____	_____
Living Expenses		
Housing	_____	_____
Food	_____	_____
Clothing	_____	_____
Transportation	_____	_____
Entertainment	_____	_____
Medical	_____	_____
Insurance	_____	_____
Children	_____	_____
Gifts	_____	_____
Miscellaneous	_____	_____
Total Expenses:	$ _____	$ _____

Cash flow margin (Savings)
(net income less total expenses): $ _____

Expense Category Descriptions

Following is a list of the kinds of expenses to consider as you complete the Expense Summary.

Charitable giving: Tithe, missionary support, and other charitable causes.

Debt payments: Credit card interest and loan payments that are not reflected in other categories.

Housing: Mortgage, rent, homeowners or renters insurance, property taxes, utilities (gas, electric, phone, trash, sewer, and water), cleaning, repairs, and maintenance.

Food: Groceries. Do not include the cost of dining out.

Clothing: Accessories and family members' wardrobes.

Transportation: Car payment, auto insurance, gas, oil, parking, repairs, and maintenance.

Entertainment: Dining out, movies, concerts, plays, sporting events, baby sitters, magazines, newspapers, vacations, club dues, and recreational activities.

Medical: Medical, dental, and vision insurance; doctor and dentist payments; and medication.

Insurance: Life insurance, disability insurance, and any other insurance (except home, auto, or medical).

Children: School lunches and supplies, lessons (such as music and dance), tuition, allowance, and child-care.

Gifts: Christmas, birthday, wedding, anniversary, and graduation presents.

Miscellaneous: Dry cleaning, laundry, animal care, hair care, toiletries, and anything not covered in the previous categories.

Cash flow margin: Money available for savings and other future financial objectives.

After completing the Expense Summary, answer the following questions:

1. If you have not done so already, determine your cash flow margin (net income less expenses) for the month which you just charted your expenses. If your cash flow was positive, what are some other uses for this money? If your cash flow was negative, in what areas can you reduce expenses?

2. Discuss what the summary reveals about your actual financial priorities.

3. What would you like your priorities to be?

4. How should your spending habits reflect your priorities?

5. Close in prayer.

Looking ahead: Think about changes you would like to make in your financial priorities. For the final project in this course, you will analyze your expenses again as you create a budget.

Remember to bring your calendar to the next session to Make a Date.

Setting Financial Goals

Setting financial goals under the guidance of the Holy Spirit gives couples direction, motivation, and hope.

W A R M • U P   15   M I N U T E S

The Way We Were

Take a few minutes to reminisce by answering these questions:

- What was your biggest financial need when you were first married?

- How has your financial situation changed since you were first married? In what ways is it the same?

- What do you think is the best purchase you have made as a couple? the worst or most disappointing?

Project Report

Share one thing you learned from last session's Home-Builders Project.

BLUEPRINTS   60 MINUTES

What Is a Goal?

A goal is a measurable and attainable objective. It is future-oriented, dependent upon you for accomplishment (although it may take an element of faith), and specific enough so that you will know when you have attained it. A goal can direct you toward accomplishing broader purposes.

If you have a large group, form smaller groups of about six people to answer the Blueprints questions. Unless otherwise noted, answer the questions in your subgroup. After finishing each section, take time for subgroups to share their answers with the whole group.

1. Which of the following statements do you think is a goal? Why?

• to be a good husband or wife

• to earn one million dollars per day by the age of thirty

• to have five quiet times per week

2. How would you describe the statements that aren't goals? What defines a goal?

Why Set Goals?

3. What are some reasons people don't set goals?

4. What is a goal you've achieved in the past? (It can be any goal.) How did setting that goal help you achieve it?

5. What do you think your financial situation will be in ten years if you set goals now and work to achieve them?

6. What is the benefit of setting financial goals?

Answer questions 7 and 8 with your spouse. After answering, you may want to share an appropriate insight or discovery with the group.

7. What is one long-term financial goal you would like to achieve?

8. What will it take for you to achieve this goal?

Steps to Setting God-Honoring Goals

Step One: *"Be filled with the Spirit."*

If you are a Christian, the Holy Spirit will never leave you. Being filled (controlled and empowered) by the Holy Spirit is a continuous process as you yield to Christ and his authority over your life. Many Christians live defeated and unproductive lives because they do not live by the power of the Spirit.

9. Read Ephesians 5:15-18. Why is it important to be "wise" and "filled with the Spirit" when making financial decisions?

Step Two: Spend time in prayer and God's Word, asking God what goals you should pursue with the financial resources he has entrusted to you.

10. What do the following verses say about what God will do for you as you spend time praying and reading his Word?

- Psalm 32:8

- Psalm 119:105

- Proverbs 3:5-6

- Matthew 7:7-8

How have these verses been true in your life?

Step Three: *Record the impressions that God is making in your life.*

11. When have you felt that God impressed upon you a decision to make or a goal to accomplish?

Step Four: *Act on the basis of faith.*

12. Read Hebrews 11:1-6. Why is faith necessary to set goals?

HomeBuilders Principle:
A faith goal is a measurable and attainable objective that you believe God wants you to move toward.

Review the steps to setting God-honoring goals.

Step One: *"Be filled with the Spirit."*

Read "Living the Christian Life" (p. 105). After reading, express your faith in silent prayer.

Step Two: *Spend time in prayer and God's Word, asking God what goals you should pursue with the financial resources he has entrusted to you.*

Ask yourself, "How am I feeling about my time in prayer and God's Word?" Set a goal to spend time in prayer and God's Word this week.

Step Three: *Record the impressions that God is making in your life.*

As a group, discuss some ways of doing this.

Step Four: *Act on the basis of faith.*

With your spouse, answer this question: What is a financial decision you're facing that requires faith?

Make a Date

Make a date with your spouse to meet before the next session to complete the HomeBuilders Project. At the next session, your leader will ask you to share one aspect of this experience.

DATE

TIME

LOCATION

HOMEBUILDERS PROJECT   6 0   M I N U T E S

As a Couple [15 minutes]

Imagine that your financial slate has been wiped clean. You have no debt or current financial obligations, and your income is equal to your current earnings. In other words, you're starting over. As a couple, assign the percentage of net income you would allocate to each of the following categories. (For a description of these categories, see page 53.)

Charitable giving   _____%

Savings (cash flow margin) _____

Housing   _____

Food   _____

Clothing   _____

Transportation   _____

Entertainment   _____

Medical   _____

Insurance   _____

Children   _____

Gifts   _____

Total: **100%**

After assigning your percentages, discuss these questions:

- Which allocation would change most if you were given a fresh start? Which would change least?

- What would be the best thing about a fresh start?

Individually [15 minutes]

1. What insight concerning financial goals did you discover in this session?

2. What are your top two or three financial goals?

3. What would you say are your spouse's top two or three financial goals?

4. Ask God what financial goals you should set, then record your impressions. As you write down what you sense God is telling you, be sure to ask yourself, "Does this glorify God?" and "Is this definitely biblical?" to ensure that you aren't confusing emotional desires with the Spirit's actual direction.

Following are some goals you may want to pray about:

- family living expenses
- paying off debt
- paying taxes
- giving
- saving

Interact as a Couple [30 minutes]

1. Discuss the questions and your impressions from the previous section.

2. Jointly set three financial goals, and list them below. Remember, goals need to be measurable and attainable. (Here is an example: Pay all credit card debt in the next eighteen months.)

3. In order to accomplish the goal, you must exercise faith by acting. Determine and record below the first step you will take toward each goal you previously listed.

4. Close your time together by praying for each other and for success in meeting your financial goals.

Remember to bring your calendar to the next session to Make a Date.

Credit, Borrowing, and Debt

A large amount of debt can prevent couples from meeting their long-term financial goals.

WARM · UP   15   MINUTES

As Advertised

Think about some memorable advertisements you have seen or heard recently. Which ad or commercial has been

- the most appealing to you?
- the worst or most obnoxious?
- the most outrageous?

What does our culture communicate about money and possessions through advertisements?

For Extra Impact

Magazine Madness: This activity will add some fun to the Warm-Up exercise. Choose a magazine to look for an ad that shows something you want, and tell the group why you would like to have that item.

Project Report

Share one thing you learned from last session's Home-Builders Project.

BLUEPRINTS   60 MINUTES

Important Definitions

Debt: Any money owed to anyone for anything; a financial obligation to someone.

Borrow: To obtain use of something belonging to someone else. (In this session, borrowing means entering into a contractual obligation to pay interest in order to use someone else's money.)

Collateral: A security (personal property, stocks,

or bonds) given as a pledge for the fulfillment of a financial obligation.

Opportunity Cost: The value of all other investment choices or alternatives forgone when making an investment decision.

Why People Borrow Money

1. What are some common reasons people borrow money (whether from a lending institution or a credit card company)? What do you think are legitimate reasons for borrowing money?

If you have a large group, form smaller groups of about six people to answer the Blueprints questions. Unless otherwise noted, answer the questions in your subgroup. After finishing each section, take time for subgroups to share their answers with the whole group.

2. In what ways has your attitude (good or bad)—or your parents' attitude—about debt influenced you as a couple?

HomeBuilders Principle:
Debt is seldom the real problem; it is symptomatic of another problem, such as greed, poor self-image, self-indulgence, impatience, or lack of self-discipline.

Scriptural Insights on Borrowing

3. What do the following verses say about borrowing money?

- Psalm 37:21

- Proverbs 22:7

- Proverbs 22:26-27

4. Under what circumstances do you think borrowing is wrong? Under what circumstances do you think it is OK?

5. Read James 4:13-14 and Luke 14:28-30. What principles can you determine from these passages?

6. How could borrowing money cause you to violate these principles?

Finances and Faith

7. Read Isaiah 55:8-9 and Philippians 4:19. How might these passages relate to money or borrowing money?

8. What is the difference between a need and a desire?

9. How has God provided for your needs in the past?

10. In what ways do you think God works in people's finances? Share a specific example if you can.

Answer questions 11 and 12 with your spouse. After answering, you may want to share an appropriate insight or discovery with the group.

11. Discuss what you'd like your debt situation to be in

- one year:

- five years:

- ten years:

What is the first step you can take to accomplish the one-year goal?

12. What is one financial decision you are considering right now? Pray together about that decision.

FYI: The Magic of Compounding

The principle of compounding has been called the eighth wonder of the world. It can either work for you or against you, depending upon whether you are a saver or a borrower. Understanding this principle can help you decide whether or not to borrow money.

For example, assume you typically have a monthly balance of $3,000 of unpaid credit card debt at 18 percent interest. If you carried this debt over the course of thirty-five years, what would be the total amount in interest you would end up paying to the credit card company?

To determine this amount, consult the chart that follows this example. Find the factor at the intersection of thirty-five years and 18 percent (328.0). Now take that factor times the average monthly credit card debt ($3,000) to calculate the compounded opportunity cost of carrying $3,000 a month in credit card debt over thirty-five years versus paying off your credit card bills each month (328.0 x $3,000 = $984,000).

To state it another way, if you invested your money in an account that earned 18 percent compounded interest, you could make an initial deposit of $3,000 and after thirty-five years you would have $984,000.

As you can see from this example, compounded interest is a powerful financial force.

YEARS WITH LOAN	INTEREST RATE						
	8%	10%	12%	14%	16%	18%	21%
5	1.5	1.6	1.7	1.9	2.1	2.3	2.6
10	2.2	2.6	3.1	3.7	4.4	5.2	6.7
15	3.2	4.2	5.5	7.1	9.3	12.0	17.5
20	4.7	6.7	9.6	13.7	19.5	27.4	45.3
25	6.9	10.8	17.0	26.5	40.9	62.7	117.4
30	10.0	17.5	30.0	50.6	85.9	143.4	304.5
35	14.8	28.1	52.7	98.1	180.3	328.0	789.8
40	21.7	45.3	93.0	188.9	378.7	750.4	1048.4

W R A P • U P   15   M I N U T E S

Read this case study, and discuss the questions that follow.

Jill: I was looking through our mail today, and I noticed that we've exceeded our limit on one of our credit card bills. Why do we owe so much?

Mike: The problem is that my commissions have been down the last six months.

Jill: So…?

Mike: So we don't have enough money coming in, and we still have a lot of bills we need to take care of every month.

Jill: What puzzles me is that last summer you were selling lots of homes and making more than enough money, and you convinced me that we needed to buy a boat. And now you're telling me that we aren't making enough for monthly expenses. Aren't your sales always down in the winter?

Mike: Yes, but I didn't think they would be down this much.

Jill: Mike, we keep falling into the same pattern we've lived by our entire marriage. We don't have a budget, we don't plan ahead, and we buy things we really don't need!

Mike: But we've enjoyed that boat! Think about how much fun we had last year with our family. Plus it gives us an opportunity to do things with the Pattersons, and you know how much *you* enjoy that.

Jill: Yes, but I *don't* enjoy being in debt! What are we going to do?

Mike: I think we just need to trust that God will bring in enough money this next summer to pay off our debt.

- What attitudes caused this couple to go into debt?
- What are some steps Mike and Jill could take to start turning their situation around?

- What have you found helpful in your marriage to deal with financial pressures in a positive way?

Make a Date

Make a date with your spouse to meet before the next session to complete the HomeBuilders Project. At the next session, your leader will ask you to share one thing from this experience.

DATE
_____

TIME
_____

LOCATION
_____

HOMEBUILDERS PROJECT   60 MINUTES

As a Couple [10 minutes]

Take a minute to consider some nonfinancial debts you owe. To whom do you owe a "debt" of gratitude or a debt of love? Think of someone, and tell each other who you are thinking about and what nonfinancial debt you owe that person.

What could you do to "pay" this person? Discuss some ideas such as sending a card or e-mail, making a phone call, or baking some cookies, and plan to follow through with a "payment" this week.

Individually [20 minutes]

Guidelines for Borrowing

Guideline One: Borrowing needs to be in accordance with God's will.

1. Read Philippians 4:6-7. When have you borrowed money, or made a financial decision, without experiencing God's peace? What was the result?

Guideline Two: Borrowing money needs to make economic sense.

2. When have you made a decision to borrow that made good sense and worked out well?

Guideline Three: *There needs to be a guaranteed way to repay the loan (a collateralized or secured loan or a job promotion, for example).*

3. Read Proverbs 22:7 and 26-27 again. What can happen to the person who borrows on a speculative basis?

Guideline Four: *You should be unified with your spouse in the decision to borrow.*

4. Read Psalm 133:1. How important is unity between a husband and wife when making a decision to borrow money? What should you do if you and your spouse disagree on a decision?

5. What is one way this session challenged you in your thinking about borrowing and debt?

6. Think of a situation when you borrowed money that you now wish you hadn't borrowed. What negative consequences did this experience have on your life? What did you learn from this experience?

7. When have you made a decision to borrow money that made good sense and worked out well?

Interact as a Couple [30 minutes]

1. Discuss your answers to the previous questions.

2. What is something you are currently considering buying on credit? Review the borrowing guidelines. How does this purchase compare with these guidelines?

3. Using the Debt Summary chart, prepare a complete summary of all money you owe. List each lender, amount owed, the date the loan will be paid off, and the payment schedule.

Debt Summary

(Date: _____)

Lender	Amount Owed	Due Date	Payment Schedule
Credit card	$3,000	NA	$25/mo
Home mortgage	$95,000	7/1/2025	$698/mo

4. Pray together over this debt list. If appropriate, set up a plan for accelerating repayment. Prioritize repaying high interest credit cards first.

If you're ready, commit to no more borrowing unless you are in complete agreement as a couple. Sign the following pledge in your spouse's personal study guide.

"I commit to you to borrow no more money nor use credit cards as a short-term loan without your complete and freely given agreement."

_____

(signature)   *(date)*

Remember to bring your calendar to the next session to Make a Date.

Giving

The key to financial freedom is giving.

W A R M • U P   15   M I N U T E S

Giving It Away

If you had one hundred thousand dollars to give away, where would you donate the money? As a couple, determine the charitable organizations you would give to and how much you would give to each. Try to come up with at least three organizations you would support.

Organization	Amount
1.	
2.	
3.	

Total: $100,000

After spreading the wealth, report to the group which organizations you gave to and why.

Project Report
Share one thing you learned from last session's Home-Builders Project.

BLUEPRINTS · 6 o MINUTES

In this session you'll learn some biblical guidelines that will help you in your decisions to give.

The Basis for Giving

If you have a large group, form smaller groups of about six people to answer the Blueprints questions. Unless otherwise noted, answer the questions in your subgroup. After finishing each section, take time for subgroups to share their answers with the whole group.

1. What factors (right or wrong) motivate people to give?

2. After each couple has chosen at least one of the following passages, read your passage with your spouse, and discuss what it says about giving. Then share your passage and insights with the group.

- Proverbs 3:9-10
- Proverbs 19:17
- Proverbs 22:9
- Proverbs 28:27
- Matthew 5:42
- Luke 6:38
- Acts 20:35

3. For another scriptural perspective on giving, read Matthew 6:19-21.

- What is the difference between earthly and heavenly treasures?

- In what ways do our giving habits reflect what we treasure?

4. Read Psalm 24:1-2. Why do you think we are sometimes reluctant to return to God what he already owns?

HomeBuilders Principle:
Giving is returning to God what he already owns.

Giving According to God's Priorities

5. What do the following passages say that some of our priorities should be?

- 1 Corinthians 16:1-2

- Galatians 2:10

- James 1:27

6. According to the previous passages, what are some practical ways you can give?

7. Read Matthew 28:18-20. If the Great Commission also reflects God's priorities, what types of ministries should you support?

8. Think about your current giving habits. Where and how much are you currently giving? How do you feel about the priorities reflected in your giving?

Answer questions 8 and 9 with your spouse. After answering, you may want to share an appropriate insight or discovery with the group.

9. Where do you think God may be leading you to give more? What other charitable causes do you think God may be leading you to support?

HomeBuilders Principle:
Giving is the result of spiritual growth, not a cause of spiritual growth.

Attitude in Giving

10. Read 2 Corinthians 8:1-5. How would you characterize the Macedonians' attitude toward giving? In comparison, how would you describe most Christians' attitude toward giving?

11. Read 2 Corinthians 9:6-8. How have you seen the principle of "reaping what you sow" in action?

12. Why should we be cheerful givers? What can you do to be a more cheerful giver?

W R A P • U P   15   M I N U T E S

Take a few minutes to review the following questions. Write down your responses to the questions you can answer. Then share your responses with the group.

- What has this group meant to you during the course of this study? Be specific.

- What is the most valuable lesson that you have learned or discovered from this study?

- How has this study changed or challenged you or your marriage?

- What would you like to see happen next for this group?

Make a Date

Make a date with your spouse to meet this week to complete the last HomeBuilders Project of this study.

DATE

TIME

LOCATION

HOMEBUILDERS PROJECT   6 0   M I N U T E S

Final Project

Now that you've reached the end of the study, the next step is to create a budget and then stick to it.

Turn to your Expense Summary from the Home-Builders Project in Session Three. Using this as a reference and asking God for guidance, decide what you should allocate to each expense category listed on the Household Budget chart.

As you work on your budget, you may also find it helpful to reference the expanded version of the Expense Summary in the Appendix (p. 139).

Some key questions you'll need to ask yourself as you work on your budget follow:

• Are we saving enough for long-term needs?

• Can we stay or get out of debt with this budget?

• What do we have to sacrifice in order to stay within this budget? Are we willing to pay that price?

Household Budget

(**Date:** _____)

Monthly Net (after taxes) Income: $ _____

Expense Category	Monthly	Other Than Monthly	Total
Charitable giving	$ _____	$_____	$_____
Debt payments	_____	_____	_____
Savings (cash flow margin)	_____	_____	_____
Living Expenses			
Housing	_____	_____	_____
Food	_____	_____	_____
Clothing	_____	_____	_____
Transportation	_____	_____	_____
Entertainment	_____	_____	_____
Medical	_____	_____	_____
Insurance	_____	_____	_____
Children	_____	_____	_____
Gifts	_____	_____	_____
Miscellaneous	_____	_____	_____
Grand Totals:	_____	_____	_____

Household Budget Category Descriptions

Following is a list of the kinds of expenses to consider as you determine your household budget.

Charitable giving: Tithe, missionary support, and other charitable causes.

Debt payments: Credit card interest and loan payments that are not reflected in other categories.

Savings: Contributions to 401Ks and IRAs and deposits to a savings account and other investments.

Housing: Mortgage, rent, homeowners or renters insurance, property taxes, utilities (gas, electric, phone, trash, sewer, and water), cleaning, repairs, and maintenance.

Food: Groceries. Do not include the cost of dining out.

Clothing: Accessories and family members' wardrobes.

Transportation: Car payment, auto insurance, gas, oil, parking, repairs, and maintenance.

Entertainment: Dining out, movies, concerts, plays, sporting events, baby sitters, magazines, newspapers, vacations, club dues, and recreational activities.

Medical: Medical, dental, and vision insurance; doctor and dentist payments; and medication.

Insurance: Life insurance, disability insurance, and any other insurance (except home, auto, or medical).

Children: School lunches and supplies, lessons (such as music and dance), tuition, allowance, and child-care.

Gifts: Christmas, birthday, wedding, anniversary, and graduation presents.

Miscellaneous: Dry cleaning, laundry, animal care, hair care, toiletries, and anything not covered in the previous categories.

For Extra Impact

Field Trip: This is a fun, hands-on experience that can help you decide where to give.

As a couple, visit a local Christian ministry that you're interested in supporting and determine

- its financial needs.
- how well it uses financial resources.
- its ministry results.
- its ministry objectives.

If visiting a ministry is not feasible, consider writing to a ministry or visiting its Web site to determine the above.

An additional financial activity you and your spouse may want to consider doing now, or in the future, is to calculate your net worth. Knowing your net worth can provide you with a financial benchmark you can use to measure your financial progress. By determining your financial net worth on a regular basis (annually, for example), you can evaluate how you are doing in reaching your overall long-term financial goals. If you are interested in doing this, work through the charts in the Appendix starting on page 142.

Please visit our Web site at www.familylife.com/homebuilders
to give us your feedback on this study and to get information
on other FamilyLife resources and conferences.

Where Do You Go From Here?

It is our prayer that you have benefited greatly from this study in the HomeBuilders Couples Series. We hope that your marriage will continue to grow as you both submit your lives to Jesus Christ and build according to his blueprints.

We also hope that you will begin reaching out to strengthen other marriages in your community and local church. Your church needs couples like you who are committed to building Christian marriages. A favorite World War II story illustrates this point very clearly.

The year was 1940. The French Army had just collapsed under Hitler's onslaught. The Dutch had folded, overwhelmed by the Nazi regime. The Belgians had surrendered. And the British Army was trapped on the coast of France in the channel port of Dunkirk.

Two hundred and twenty thousand of Britain's finest young men seemed doomed to die, turning the English Channel red with their blood. The Fuehrer's troops, only miles away in the hills of France, didn't realize how close to victory they actually were.

Any rescue seemed feeble and futile in the time remaining. A "thin" British Navy—"the professionals"—told King George VI that at best they could save 17,000 troops. The House of Commons was warned to prepare for "hard and heavy tidings."

Politicians were paralyzed. The king was powerless. And the Allies could only watch as spectators from a distance. Then as the doom of the British Army seemed imminent, a strange fleet appeared on the horizon of the English Channel—the wildest assortment of boats perhaps ever assembled in history.

Trawlers, tugs, scows, fishing sloops, lifeboats, pleasure craft, smacks and coasters, sailboats, even the London fire-brigade flotilla. *Each ship was manned by civilian volunteers—English fathers sailing to rescue Britain's exhausted, bleeding sons.*

William Manchester writes in his epic novel, *The Last Lion*, that even today what happened in 1940 in less than twenty-four hours seems like a miracle—not only were all of the British soldiers rescued, but 118,000 other Allied troops as well.

Today the Christian home is much like those troops at Dunkirk. Pressured, trapped, and demoralized, it needs help. Your help. The Christian community may be much like England—we stand waiting for politicians, professionals, even for our pastors to step in and save the family. But the problem is much larger than all of those combined can solve.

With the highest divorce rate of any nation on earth, we need an all-out effort by men and women "sailing" to rescue the exhausted and wounded family casualties. We need an outreach effort by common couples with faith in an uncommon God. For too long, married couples within the church have abdicated the privilege and responsibility of influencing others to those in full-time vocational ministry.

Possibly this study has indeed been used to "light the torch" of your spiritual lives. Perhaps it was already burning, and this provided more fuel. Regardless, may we challenge you to invest your lives in others?

You and other couples around the world can team together to build thousands of marriages and families. By starting a HomeBuilders group, you will not only strengthen other marriages but you will also see your marriage grow as you share these principles with others.

Will You Join Us in "Touching Lives...Changing Families"?

The following are some practical ways you can make a difference in families today:

1. Gather a group of four to eight couples, and lead them through the six sessions of this HomeBuilders study, *Mastering Money in Your Marriage*. (Why not consider challenging others in your church or community to form additional HomeBuilders groups?)

2. Commit to continue marriage building by doing another course in the HomeBuilders Couples Series.

3. An excellent outreach tool is the film *"JESUS,"* which is available on video. For more information, contact FamilyLife at 1-800-FL-TODAY.

4. Host a dinner party. Invite families from your neighborhood to your home, and as a couple share your faith in Christ.

5. Reach out and share the love of Christ with neighborhood children.

6. If you have attended the FamilyLife Marriage Conference, why not offer to assist your pastor in counseling couples engaged to be married, using the material you received?

For more information about any of the above ministry opportunities, contact your local church, or write:

> **FamilyLife**
> P.O. Box 8220
> Little Rock, AR 72221-8220
> 1-800-FL-TODAY
> **www.familylife.com**

Our Problems, God's Answers

Every couple eventually has to deal with problems in marriage. Communication problems. Money problems. Difficulties with sexual intimacy. These issues are important to cultivating a strong, loving relationship with your spouse. The HomeBuilders Couples Series is designed to help you strengthen your marriage in many of these critical areas.

Part One: The Big Problem

One basic problem is at the heart of every other problem in every marriage, and it's a problem we can't help you fix. No matter how hard you try, this is one problem that is too big for you to deal with on your own.

The problem is separation from God. If you want to experience marriage the way it was designed to be, you need a vital relationship with the God who created you and offers you the power to live a life of joy and purpose.

And what separates us from God is one more problem—sin. Most of us have assumed throughout our lives that the term "sin" refers to a list of bad habits that everyone agrees are wrong. We try to deal with our sin problem by working hard to become better people. We read books to learn how to control our anger, or we resolve to stop cheating on our taxes.

But in our hearts, we know our sin problem runs much deeper than a list of bad habits. All of us have rebelled against God. We have ignored him and have decided to run our own lives in a way that makes sense to us. The Bible says that the God who created us wants us to follow his plan for our lives. But because of our sin problem, we think our ideas and plans are better than his.

- *"For all have sinned and fall short of the glory of God"* (Romans 3:23).

What does it mean to "fall short of the glory of God"? It means that none of us has trusted and treasured God the way we should. We have sought to satisfy ourselves with other things and have treated those things as more valuable than God. We have gone our own way. According to the Bible, we have to pay a penalty for our sin. We cannot simply do things the way we choose and hope it will all be OK with God. Following our own plan leads to our destruction.

- *"There is a way that seems right to a man, but in the end it leads to death"* (Proverbs 14:12).

- *"For the wages of sin is death"* (Romans 6:23a).

The penalty for sin is that we are forever separated from God's love. God is holy, and we are sinful. No matter how hard we try, we cannot come up with some plan, like living a good life or even trying to do what the Bible says, and hope that we can avoid the penalty.

God's Solution to Sin

Thankfully God has a way to solve our dilemma. He became a man through the person of Jesus Christ. He lived a holy life, in perfect obedience to God's plan. He also willingly died on a cross to pay our penalty for sin. Then he proved that he is more powerful than sin or death by rising from the dead. He alone has the power to overrule the penalty for our sin.

- *"Jesus answered, 'I am the way and the truth and the life. No one comes to the Father except through me'"* (John 14:6).

- *"But God demonstrates his own love for us in this: While we were still sinners, Christ died for us"* (Romans 5:8).

- *"Christ died for our sins...he was buried...he was raised on the third day according to the Scriptures...he appeared to Peter, and then to the Twelve. After that, he appeared to more than five hundred"* (1 Corinthians 15:3-6).

- *"For the wages of sin is death, but the gift of God is eternal life in Christ Jesus our Lord"* (Romans 6:23).

The death of Jesus has fixed our sin problem. He has bridged the gap between God and us. He is calling all of us to come to him and to give up our own flawed plan for how to run our lives. He wants us to trust God and his plan.

Accepting God's Solution

If you agree that you are separated from God, he is calling you to confess your sins. All of us have made messes of our lives because we have stubbornly preferred our ideas and plans over his. As a result, we deserve to be cut off from God's love and his care for us. But God has promised that if we will agree that we have rebelled against his plan for us and have messed up our lives, he will forgive us and will fix our sin problem.

- *"Yet to all who received him, to those who believed in his name, he gave the right to become children of God"* (John 1:12).

- *"For it is by grace you have been saved, through faith—and this not from yourselves, it is the gift of*

God—not by works, so that no one can boast"
(Ephesians 2:8-9).

When the Bible talks about receiving Christ, it means we acknowledge that we are sinners and that we can't fix the problem ourselves. It means we turn away from our sin. And it means we trust Christ to forgive our sins and to make us the kind of people he wants us to be. It's not enough to just intellectually believe that Christ is the Son of God. We must trust in him and his plan for our lives by faith, as an act of the will.

Are things right between you and God, with him and his plan at the center of your life? Or is life spinning out of control as you seek to make your way on your own?

You can decide today to make a change. You can turn to Christ and allow him to transform your life. All you need to do is to talk to him and tell him what is stirring in your mind and in your heart. If you've never done this before, considering taking the steps listed here:

- Do you agree that you need God? Tell God.

- Have you made a mess of your life by following your own plan? Tell God.

- Do you want God to forgive you? Tell God.

- Do you believe that Jesus' death on the cross and his resurrection from the dead gave him the power to fix your sin problem and to grant you the gift of eternal life? Tell God.

- Are you ready to acknowledge that God's plan for your life is better than any plan you could come up with? Tell God.

- Do you agree that God has the right to be the Lord and master of your life? Tell God.

"Seek the Lord while he may be found;
call on him while he is near"
(Isaiah 55:6).

Following is a suggested prayer:

Lord Jesus, I need you. Thank you for dying on the cross
for my sins. I receive you as my Savior and Lord. Thank
you for forgiving my sins and giving me eternal life.
Make me the kind of person you want me to be.

Does this prayer express the desire of your heart? If it does, pray it right now, and Christ will come into your life, as he promised.

Part Two: Living the Christian Life

For a person who is a follower of Christ—a Christian—the penalty for sin is paid in full. But the effect of sin continues throughout our lives.

- *"If we claim to be without sin, we deceive ourselves and the truth is not in us"* (1 John 1:8).

- *"For what I do is not the good I want to do; no, the evil I do not want to do—this I keep on doing"* (Romans 7:19).

The effects of sin carry over into our marriages as well. Even Christians struggle to maintain solid, God-honoring marriages. Most couples eventually realize that they can't do it on their own. But with God's help, they can succeed. The Holy Spirit can have a huge impact in the marriages of Christians who live constantly, moment by moment, under his gracious direction.

Self-Centered Christians

Many Christians struggle to live the Christian life in their own strength because they are not allowing God to control their lives. Their interests are self-directed, often resulting in failure and frustration.

- *"Brothers, I could not address you as spiritual but as worldly—mere infants in Christ. I gave you milk, not solid food, for you were not yet ready for it. Indeed, you are still not ready. You are still worldly. For since there is jealousy and quarreling among you, are you not worldly? Are you not acting like mere men?"* (1 Corinthians 3:1-3).

The self-centered Christian cannot experience the abundant and fruitful Christian life. Such people trust in their own efforts to live the Christian life: They are either uninformed about—or have forgotten—God's love, forgiveness, and power. This kind of Christian

- has an up-and-down spiritual experience.

- cannot understand himself—he wants to do what is right, but cannot.

- fails to draw upon the power of the Holy Spirit to live the Christian life.

Some or all of the following traits may characterize the Christian who does not fully trust God:

disobedience	plagued by impure thoughts
lack of love for God and others	jealous
	worrisome
inconsistent prayer life	easily discouraged, frustrated
lack of desire for Bible study	critical
legalistic attitude	lack of purpose

Note: The individual who professes to be a Christian but who continues to practice sin should realize that he may not be a Christian at all, according to 1 John 2:3, 3:6, 9 and Ephesians 5:5.

Spirit-Centered Christians

When a Christian puts Christ on the throne of his life, he yields to God's control. This Christian's interests are directed by the Holy Spirit, resulting in harmony with God's plan.

- *"But the fruit of the Spirit is love, joy, peace, patience, kindness, goodness, faithfulness, gentleness and self-control. Against such things there is no law"* (Galatians 5:22-23).

Jesus said:

- *"I have come that they may have life, and have it to the full"* (John 10:10b).

- *"I am the vine; you are the branches. If a man remains in me and I in him, he will bear much fruit; apart from me you can do nothing"* (John 15:5).

- *"But you will receive power when the Holy Spirit comes on you; and you will be my witnesses in Jerusalem, and in all Judea and Samaria, and to the ends of the earth"* (Acts 1:8).

The following traits result naturally from the Holy Spirit's work in our lives:

Christ centered	love
Holy Spirit empowered	joy
motivated to tell others about Jesus	peace
	patience
dedicated to prayer	kindness
student of God's Word	goodness
trusts God	faithfulness
obeys God	gentleness
	self-control

The degree to which these traits appear in a Christian's life and marriage depends upon the extent to which the Christian trusts the Lord with every detail of life, and upon that person's maturity in Christ. One who is only beginning to understand the ministry of the Holy Spirit should not be discouraged if he is not as fruitful as mature Christians who have known and experienced this truth for a longer period of time.

Giving God Control

Jesus promises his followers an abundant and fruitful life as they allow themselves to be directed and empowered by the Holy Spirit. As we give God control of our lives, Christ lives in and through us in the power of the Holy Spirit (John 15).

If you sincerely desire to be directed and empowered by God, you can turn your life over to the control of the Holy Spirit right now (Matthew 5:6; John 7:37-39).

First, confess your sins to God, agreeing with him that you want to turn from any past sinful patterns in your life. Thank God in faith that he has forgiven all of your sins because Christ died for you (Colossians 2:13-15; 1 John 1:9; 2:1-3; Hebrews 10:1-18).

Be sure to offer every area of your life to God (Romans 12:1-2). Consider what areas you might rather keep to yourself, and be sure you're willing to give God control in those areas.

By faith, commit yourself to living according to the Holy Spirit's guidance and power.

- *Live by the Spirit:* "*So I say, live by the Spirit, and you will not gratify the desires of the sinful nature. For the sinful nature desires what is contrary to the Spirit, and the Spirit what is contrary to the sinful nature. They are in conflict with each other, so that you do not do what you want*" (Galatians 5:16-17).

- *Trust in God's Promise:* "*This is the confidence we have in approaching God: that if we ask anything according to his will, he hears us. And if we know that he hears us—whatever we ask—we know that we have what we asked of him*" (1 John 5:14-15).

Expressing Your Faith Through Prayer

Prayer is one way of expressing your faith to God. If the prayer that follows expresses your sincere desire, consider praying the prayer or putting the thoughts into your own words:

Dear God, I need you. I acknowledge that I have been directing my own life and that, as a result, I have sinned against you. I thank you that you have forgiven my sins through Christ's death on the cross for me. I now invite Christ to take his place on the throne of my life. Take control of my life through the Holy Spirit as you promised you would if I asked in faith. I now thank you for directing my life and for empowering me through the Holy Spirit.

Walking in the Spirit

If you become aware of an area of your life (an attitude or an action) that is displeasing to God, simply confess your sin, and thank God that he has forgiven your sins on the basis of Christ's death on the cross. Accept God's love and forgiveness by faith, and continue to have fellowship with him.

If you find that you've taken back control of your life through sin—a definite act of disobedience—try this exercise, "Spiritual Breathing," as you give that control back to God.

1. Exhale. Confess your sin. Agree with God that you've sinned against him, and thank him for his forgiveness of it, according to 1 John 1:9 and Hebrews 10:1-25. Remember that confession involves repentance, a determination to change attitudes and actions.

2. Inhale. Surrender control of your life to Christ, inviting the Holy Spirit to once again take charge. Trust that he now directs and empowers you, according to the command of Galatians 5:16-17 and the promise of 1 John 5:14-15. Returning to your faith in God enables you to continue to experience God's love and forgiveness.

Revolutionizing Your Marriage

This new commitment of your life to God will enrich your marriage. Sharing with your spouse what you've committed to is a powerful step in solidifying this commitment. As you exhibit the Holy Spirit's work within you, your spouse may be drawn to make the same commitment you've made. If both of you have given control of your lives to the Holy Spirit, you'll be able to help each other remain true to God, and your marriage may be revolutionized. With God in charge of your lives, life becomes an amazing adventure.

Leader's Notes

Contents

About Leading a HomeBuilders Group

What is the leader's job?

Your role is that of "facilitator"—one who encourages people to think and to discover what Scripture says, who helps group members feel comfortable, and who keeps things moving forward.

What is the best setting and time schedule for this study?

This study is designed as a small-group home Bible study. However, it can be adapted for use in a Sunday school setting as well. Here are some suggestions for using this study in a small group and in a Sunday school class:

In a small group

To create a friendly and comfortable atmosphere, it is recommended that you do this study in a home setting. In many cases, the couple that leads the study also serves as host to the group. Sometimes involving another couple as host is a good idea. Choose the option you believe will work best for your group, taking into account factors such as the number of couples participating and the location.

Each session is designed as a ninety-minute study, but we recommend a two-hour block of time. This will allow you to move through each part of the study at a more relaxed pace. However, be sure to keep in mind one of the cardinal rules of a small group: Good groups start *and* end on time. People's time is valuable, and your group will appreciate your being respectful of this.

In a Sunday school class

There are two important adaptations you need to make if you want to use this study in a class setting: (1) The material you cover should focus on the content from the Blueprints section of each session. Blueprints is the heart of each session and is designed to last sixty minutes. (2) Most Sunday school classes are taught in a teacher format instead of a small-group format. If this study will be used in a class setting, the class should adapt to a small-group dynamic. This will involve an interactive, discussion-based format and may also require a class to break into multiple smaller groups (we recommend groups of six to eight people).

What is the best size group?

We recommend from four to eight couples (including you and your spouse). If you have more people interested than you think you can accommodate, consider asking someone else to lead a second group. If you have a large group, you are encouraged at various times in the study to break into smaller subgroups. This helps you cover the material in a timely fashion and allows for optimum interaction and participation within the group.

What about refreshments?

Many groups choose to serve refreshments, which help create an environment of fellowship. If you plan on including refreshments in your study, here are a couple of suggestions: (1) For the first session (or two) you should provide the refreshments and then allow the group to be involved by having people sign up to bring them on later dates. (2) Consider starting your group with a short time of informal fellowship and refreshments (fifteen minutes), then move into the study. If couples are late, they miss only the food and don't disrupt the study. You may also want to have refreshments available at the end of your meeting to encourage fellowship, but remember, respect the group members' time by ending the study on schedule and allowing anyone who needs to leave right away the opportunity to do so gracefully.

What about child care?

Groups handle this differently depending on their needs. Here are a couple of options you may want to consider:

- Have group members be responsible for making their own arrangements.

- As a group, hire child care, and have all the kids watched in one location.

What about prayer?

An important part of a small group is prayer. However, as the leader, you need to be sensitive to the level of comfort the people in your group have toward praying in front of others. Never call on people to pray aloud if you don't know if they are comfortable doing this. There are a number of creative approaches you can take, such as modeling prayer, calling for volunteers, and letting people state their prayers in the form of finishing a sentence. A tool that is helpful in a group is a prayer list. You are encouraged to do this, but let it be someone else's ministry to the group. You should lead the prayer time, but allow another couple in the group the opportunity to create, update, and distribute prayer lists.

In closing

An excellent resource that covers leading a HomeBuilders group in greater detail is the *HomeBuilders Leader Guide* by Drew and Kit Coons. This book may be obtained at your local Christian bookstore or by contacting Group Publishing or FamilyLife.

About the Leader's Notes

The sessions in this study can be easily led without a lot of preparation time. However, accompanying Leader's Notes have been provided to assist you in preparation. The categories within the Leader's Notes are as follows:

Objectives

The purpose of the Objectives is to help focus on the issues that will be presented in each session.

Notes and Tips

This section will relate any general comments about the session. This information should be viewed as ideas, helps, and suggestions. You may want to create a checklist of things you want to be sure to do in each session.

Commentary

Included in this section are notes that relate specifically to Blueprints questions. Not all Blueprints questions in each session will have accompanying commentary notes. Questions with related commentaries are designated by numbers (for example, Blueprints question 3 in Session One would correspond to number 3 in the Commentary section of Session One Leader's Notes).

Session One:
Putting Money in Its Place

Objectives

Managing money wisely is a challenge for any couple, regardless of income level.

In this session, couples will...

• evaluate their view of money.

• study the parable of the rich fool.

• examine their financial needs.

Notes and Tips

1. If you have not already done so, read "About the Sessions" on pages 4 and 5 as well as "About Leading a HomeBuilders Group" and "About the Leader's Notes" starting on page 112.

2. To further equip yourself to lead this course, you may want to read Ron Blue's book, *Master Your Money*. This book provides additional material on the topics discussed in this study.

3. As part of the first session, you may want to review with the group some Ground Rules (see page 11 in the Introduction).

4. Be sure you have a study guide for each person. You will also need extra Bibles and pens or pencils.

5. This first session includes the Numbers Game, which is a "For Extra Impact" exercise that your group can use as an additional Warm-Up activity.

Part of the fun of the Numbers Game is to see the different approaches group members take to complete this exercise. This is similar to the way couples approach finances differently. There are always alternative ways to spend money. However, approaching these alternatives without a plan—as many people do—usually results in frustration and confusion. Having a plan helps you sort through the alternatives to meet your own unique financial needs.

The secret to the Numbers Game is to recognize and follow the pattern. The numbers are divided into four quadrants: number one is in the upper left, number two is in the upper right, number three is in the lower left, and number four is in the lower right. This pattern repeats itself until you reach the last number, ninety.

If you use this exercise, be sure to time it so that the session stays on track.

6. Because this is the first session, make a special point to tell the group about the importance of the HomeBuilders Project. Encourage couples to "Make a Date" to complete the project before the next meeting. Mention that you will ask them to share something they learned during the next session's Warm-Up.

7. A note at the start of Blueprints recommends forming smaller groups. This is done for two reasons: (1) to help facilitate discussion and participation by everyone, and (2) to help you get through the material in the allotted time.

8. Because this is the first session, consider offering a closing prayer instead of asking others to pray aloud. Many people are uncomfortable praying in front of others, and unless you already know your group well, it may be wise to slowly venture into various methods of prayer. Regardless of how you decide to close, you should serve as the model.

9. With this group just getting under way, you may want to remind the group that it's not too late to invite another couple to join the group. Challenge group members to think about couples they could invite to the next session.

10. Start the session on time, even if everyone is not present. Briefly share a few positive feelings about leading this study:

- Express your interest in strengthening your own marriage and becoming a better financial manager.

- Admit that your marriage and your method of managing money are not perfect.

- If applicable, mention that the concepts in this study have been helpful in your marriage.

- Recognize that various individuals or couples may have been reluctant to come.

- Thank group members for their interest and willingness to participate.

- Distribute the study guides if you have not already done so, and give a quick overview of this study. The group members need to know how they are going to benefit personally. They also need to know where this course will take them, especially if they are apprehensive about being a part of this study.

Commentary

Here is additional information about the Blueprints questions. The numbers that follow correspond to the numbers of the questions in the Blueprints. If you share any of these points, be sure to do so in a manner that does not stifle discussion by making you the authority with *the real answers.* Begin your comments by saying statements such as "One thing I notice in this passage is…" or "I think another reason for this is…"

Notes are not included for every question. Many of the questions in this study are designed for group members to answer according to their own opinions and experiences.

1. If your group needs help starting the discussion, here are some suggestions: staying out of debt, planning and sticking to a budget, living on one or two incomes, credit card abuse, and saving for the future.

3. Christian couples also wonder how much they should give, who to give to, and whether they have the right attitude about money.

5. You might want to state that the remainder of the study will address some of these questions.

9. The rich man thought he was secure and significant, but he was mistaken and came under God's judgment. It may be helpful to define these two terms: Security means safety and dependability; significance means importance and meaningfulness.

10. Success is not defined by one's financial resources.

Attention HomeBuilders Leaders

FamilyLife invites you to register your HomeBuilders group. Your registration connects you to the HomeBuilders Leadership Network, a worldwide movement of couples who are using HomeBuilders to strengthen marriages and families in their communities. You'll receive the latest news about HomeBuilders and other ministry opportunities to help strengthen marriages and families in your community. As the HomeBuilders Leadership Network grows, we will offer additional resources such as online training, prayer requests, and chat with authors. There is no cost or obligation to register; simply go to www.familylife.com/homebuilders.

Session Two:
Stewardship

Objectives

Stewardship is managing God's resources to accomplish God-given goals.

In this session, couples will...

• discuss attitudes toward money.

• look at biblical examples of stewardship.

• evaluate their personal stewardship of God's resources.

Notes and Tips

1. The main point of this session is that God owns everything. As stewards of God's resources, we are responsible for our use of all that has been entrusted to us.

2. Since this is the second session, your group members have probably warmed up a bit to each other, but may not yet feel free to be completely open and honest about their marriage relationships. Don't force the issue. Continue to encourage couples to attend and to complete their projects.

3. If someone joins the group for the first time this session, give a brief summary of Session One's main points. Also, be sure to introduce those who do not know each other, and have couples pass their books around again to record names, phone numbers, and e-mail addresses.

4. If you told the group members during the first session that you would ask them to share something they learned from the first HomeBuilders Project, be sure to ask them. This is an important time for you to establish an environment of accountability.

5. For the Wrap-Up exercise in this session, the group will form three teams to manage various assets of the Kingdom Corporation. Each team will need one asset to manage. The assets include: (1) $1 million, (2) the Kingdom Corporation facility (a 100,000 square-foot multiuse facility), and (3) the Kingdom Corporation fleet (a dozen brand-new minivans). You can either assign these assets or have teams draw for them.

Tell the teams there are no restrictions or limitations to what they can do with their Kingdom Corporation assets. However they decide to use the assets is fine, but the owner will want an accounting of their decisions.

6. If you're planning to have refreshments, make sure the arrangements have been made.

7. If your group has decided to use a prayer list, make sure this is covered.

8. For the closing prayer in this session, you may want to ask one or two volunteers to close the group in prayer. Before this session, check with a couple of people who would be comfortable praying aloud.

Commentary

Note: The numbers that follow correspond to the Blueprints questions of the same numbers in the session.

1. Many people have no guidelines other than trying to keep one step ahead.

2. As people respond to this question, pay attention to the level of understanding within the group. Are they all familiar with the biblical teaching on stewardship, or do their answers indicate otherwise?

4. These verses show that God owns everything in the world, including all that is in our possession.

5. To bring gain to the master by using what he entrusted to them.

8. You may want to share that God rewards us according to faithfulness not according to amount. Whether we have little money or great sums, our stewardship is measured by our loving obedience.

9. Faithfulness with "worldly wealth"—yours or someone else's—can be a prerequisite to God entrusting you with "true riches."

Session Three:
Financial Priorities

Objectives

Every financial decision you make is ultimately a spiritual decision about how God would like you to prioritize your money.

In this session, couples will...

- discuss various influences on their financial priorities.

- identify biblical priorities for money management.

- evaluate their approach to establishing financial priorities.

Notes and Tips

1. Congratulations! After completing this session, you will be halfway through this study. It's time for a checkup: How are you feeling? How is the group going? What has worked well so far? What things might you consider changing as you begin the second half?

2. This session will help couples realize that financial decisions are really priority decisions. Money is merely a tool used to meet the real priorities of life, thus its use reflects what a person—and a couple—considers to be truly important.

3. Blueprints question eight directs couples to look up different Scripture passages. This approach allows the group to look at multiple passages simultaneously, saves time, and gives the group members the opportunity to learn from one another.

4. The Wrap-Up exercise should be enjoyable for couples, although there is a potential for conflict. It will be interesting for couples to notice how they arrive at their decisions. In some cases, one person will take the lead and push his or her priorities on the other, or one person may consistently defer to the other's wishes. The point is for couples to realize that each partner in a marriage will have his or her own priorities, which can cause misunderstanding and conflict.

5. The HomeBuilders Project for this session is an important part of this course. Couples will complete an Expense Summary that will help them to evaluate their financial priorities and aid later in establishing a budget (the HomeBuilders Project in Session Six).

As an example to the group, it is important that you and your spouse complete the HomeBuilders Project for each session.

6. Remember the importance of starting and ending on time.

7. Greet people as they arrive. Share personal expressions of appreciation for everyone's participation and support in earlier sessions. Express your appreciation for the opportunity to get to know them better. Start the session on time.

Commentary

1. The world urges us to spend money on things that do not matter—things that are not eternal. We use our money to buy possessions that give us esteem in the eyes of our friends.

3. If most people rank God first, focus on what they listed next.

Note: The numbers that follow correspond to the Blueprints questions of the same numbers in the session.

6. To add to the effectiveness of this question, suggest that each couple think of a significant item they might purchase, such as furniture, an appliance, a vehicle, or a vacation. Declare that the husband wants to make the purchase, but the wife disagrees on the need, expense, or style of the item. Then ask, "How do you resolve this disagreement?" Have couples talk together for a few minutes about how they would handle the matter. Then encourage couples to share their most likely approach to resolving this disagreement.

7. In regards to the second part of this question, you may want to instruct group members each to first write down ways in which their financial priorities differ from those of their spouses. After a minute or two, ask couples to compare what they wrote.

In many cases, a financial disagreement is an indicator of differing priorities. In other cases, the disagreement may be a smoke screen for another, often unrelated, problem.

10. Psalm 37:21: Repay all debts.
Proverbs 3:9: Honor God with what you have (give).
Proverbs 31:16: Save in anticipation of future needs.
Romans 13:6-7: Pay taxes.
1 Timothy 5:8: Provide for your household (living expenses).

12. Encourage people to suggest specific examples as they respond. (For example, deciding to use a credit card to dine out instead of cooking at home may reduce the amount of money available to put in the vacation fund at the end of the month.)

Session Four:
Setting Financial Goals

Objectives

Setting financial goals under the guidance of the Holy Spirit gives couples direction, motivation, and hope.

In this session, couples will...

• define what a goal is.

• discuss the value of setting financial goals.

• examine four steps in setting goals.

• discover how to ensure that financial goal setting is guided by the Holy Spirit.

Notes and Tips

1. Session Four leads couples toward setting specific financial goals for the future. This process requires understanding the difference between purposes and goals.

A purpose statement describes a broad intention or direction in which to move. A goal is a specifically measurable and attainable objective related to that purpose.

2. The Blueprints section includes a discussion about the Holy Spirit. If you sense that this is an unfamiliar subject for anyone in your group, you may want to spend some time explaining who the Holy Spirit is and how the Spirit works in a Christian's life. A good way of doing this is to share from your own life.

Also, as part of the Wrap-Up, the group will be directed to read "Living the Christian Life" on page 105. This provides Scriptures and information about the Holy Spirit.

If you think someone in your group has questions about what a Christian is, this might be a good time to spend a few minutes explaining how you became a Christian and the difference that Christ has made in your life. You can also refer group members to "The Big Problem" (p. 101).

3. By this time, group members should be more comfortable with each other. For prayer at the end of this session, you may want to give everyone an opportunity to pray by asking the group to finish a sentence like this: "Lord, I want to thank you for..." Be sensitive to anyone who may not feel comfortable doing this.

4. You may want to make some notes right after the meeting to help you evaluate how this session went. Ask yourself questions such as: Did everyone participate? Do I need to make a special effort to follow up with anyone before the next session? Asking yourself questions like these will help you stay focused.

5. You and your spouse may want to write notes of thanks and encouragement to the couples in your group this week. Thank them for their commitment and contribution to the group, and let them know that you are praying for them. Make a point to pray for them as you write their notes.

Commentary

Note: The numbers that follow correspond to the Blueprints questions of the same numbers in the session.

1. If there is not a consensus to the answer of this question, refer the group to the definition under "What Is a Goal?"

2. "Nongoals" could be classified as purpose statements, wants, desires, or just wishful thinking.

3. Many people lack the discipline. Or they try and fail, and then give up.

6. In response to this question, you may want to share a personal example from your own life.

9. Only those who have consciously surrendered control of their lives to the Holy Spirit can be guided by the Spirit to set God-honoring financial goals. Without the guidance of the Spirit, we are left to flounder in uncertainty about what truly is the best direction for us to follow.

10. Psalm 32:8: God will instruct, teach, counsel, and watch over you.
Psalm 119:105: God's Word provides enlightenment.
Proverbs 3:5-6: God can make the way clear.
Matthew 7:7-8: Be persistent in prayer.

As you spend time in the Word and in prayer, the Holy Spirit will begin to guide you in setting specific, attainable financial goals.

As you consider what you sense God is telling you through prayer and the Word, be sure to ask yourself, "Does this glorify

God?" or "Is this definitely biblical?" to ensure you're not
confusing emotional desires with the Spirit's actual direction.

12. As Hebrews 11:6 says, "Without faith it is impossible to
please God."

Session Five:
Credit, Borrowing, and Debt

Objectives

A large amount of debt can prevent couples from meeting their long-term financial goals.

In this session, couples will...

• identify reasons why people borrow money.

• examine Scriptures related to borrowing money.

• explore guidelines to follow in deciding whether or not to borrow money.

Notes and Tips

1. Many couples today find it too easy to fall into debt and credit problems. This session is designed to help group members realize the attitudes that cause them to go into debt, discover how debt hurts them in the future, and learn some guidelines to follow when making decisions about borrowing.

2. If you choose to do the "For Extra Impact" exercise, you will need a supply of magazines for the group. Ideally, each person should have one magazine. You may want to ask everyone to bring a magazine to this session.

3. As the leader of this small group, one of the best things you can do for your group is to pray specifically for each group member. Take some time to pray as you prepare for this session.

4. *Looking ahead:* For the next session—the last session of this study—you may want to have someone, or a couple, share what this study or group has meant to him or her. If this is something you would like to do, think about who you will ask to share.

Commentary

3. Psalm 37:21: Those who do not repay debts are wicked.

Proverbs 22:7: A person who borrows is under the control of the lender.

Proverbs 22:26-27: Entering into obligations without having the means to repay leads to losing what you have.

Note: The numbers that follow correspond to the Blueprints questions of the same numbers in the session.

4. Psalm 37:21 says that failing to repay a debt is wicked. But nowhere in Scripture is borrowing called a sin. Romans 13:8, which says, "Let no debt remain outstanding," is sometimes interpreted that borrowing money is sinful. However, the context of this verse is human relationships, not specifically financial transactions. The debt that is mentioned could include finances, but not necessarily. In addition, some would say that the outstanding debt mentioned in Romans 13:8 refers only to agreed upon payments that have not been made.

We should keep in mind that anytime someone enters a lender/debtor relationship, the original relationship changes. Therefore, the principle of not owing money to others is a good one, but it is not a commandment forbidding us to borrow money.

Generally, borrowing to increase one's ability to earn money—a college education—or to purchase an asset that increases in value—a home—can make economic sense. Most people fall prey to the pitfalls of debt when they borrow money to provide instant gratification of a want (a vacation, new car, or a particular consumer good, for example).

5. Following are a couple of perspectives you might want to share: Do not take the future for granted because you have no idea what will happen. Count the cost before you enter into a financial commitment.

   In addition, invite suggestions about which costs need to be counted before borrowing money, such as the amount borrowed, the interest, the lost income that could have been generated with that money, and the pressure of having an obligation to repay.

6. When you borrow money, you do so with the presumption that you will be able to pay it back in the future. But in reality you have no idea what will happen in the future and whether you will actually be able to repay the debt.

Session Six:
Giving

Objectives

The key to financial freedom is giving.

In this session, couples will...

• look at reasons for giving.

• study Scriptures that present helpful principles for giving.

• evaluate their experience in this course.

Notes and Tips

1. Tithing is not directly addressed in this session. This is intentional to avoid the trap many strict tithers fall into of separating their money into "God's portion" and "my portion." The reality is that it all belongs to God. Giving is intended to be a reflection of God's ownership, not a contribution from our own possessions.

2. The final HomeBuilders Project for this course is creating a household budget. This is an important step for couples in their quest to master money in their marriages. Although the course ends with this study, encourage couples to invest in doing the final project. The reward could pay dividends for years to come!

Because accountability is important, and as an act of encouragement, you may wish to follow up with group members in a couple of weeks to see if they completed the Final Project from this session.

3. While this HomeBuilders Couples Series has great value, people are likely to return to previous patterns of living unless they commit to a plan for continuing the progress they've made. During this final session, encourage couples to take specific steps beyond this series to keep growing in their marriages. For example, you may want to challenge couples who have developed the habit of a "date night" during the course of this study to continue this practice. Also, you may want the group to consider doing another study from this series.

4. During this last session, you may want to consider devoting some time to plan for one more meeting—a party to celebrate the completion of this study!

5. At the end of this session, you'll find a "For Extra Impact" exercise as well as a note about creating a net worth statement. While both of these activities are optional, you may want to encourage the couples in your group to consider doing one or both of these activities.

Commentary

Note: The numbers that follow correspond to the Blueprints questions of the same numbers in the session.

1. If helpful to the discussion, interject the following examples of wrong and right motives: Wrong motives include desire for recognition, desire to please another person, and desire to receive something in return. Right motives include a love for God, gratefulness for God's provision, a desire to show God's love, and a desire to serve and help others.

3. The statement "where your treasure is, there your heart will be also" is critically important and often misunderstood. Where we place our treasure is a reflection of our heart attitude, not a cause of our heart attitude.

Taking a look at where we put our treasures is a good indicator of whether we are depending on earthly or heavenly treasure to provide peace and security.

4. Many people refuse to acknowledge God's ownership of all they have. We also tend to be selfish with the things that God has graciously loaned to us.

5. 1 Corinthians 16:1-2: Aiding other believers who are in need.
Galatians 2:10: Aiding the poor.
James 1:27: Aiding widows and orphans—those who cannot help themselves.

7. Giving should assist evangelism and discipleship around the world.

Recommended Reading

Generous Living, Ron Blue

A Life Well Spent, Russ Crosson

Master Your Money, Ron Blue

Money and Your Marriage, Russ Crosson

Money Talks and So Can We, Ron and Judy Blue

Raising Money-Smart Kids, Ron and Judy Blue

The Secret, Bill Bright

Taming the Money Monster, Ron Blue

Appendix

Expense Summary (expanded version)

(**For:** _____/_____)
          month,   year

Net Income (after taxes): $ _____

Expense Category	Amount Paid Last Month	Usual Monthly Cost
Charitable giving		
Tithe	$ _____	$ _____
Missions support	_____	_____
Other	_____	_____
Total Charitable giving:	_____	_____
Debt payments		
Credit card interest	_____	_____
Loan payments	_____	_____
Other	_____	_____
Total Debt payment:	_____	_____
Savings (cash flow margin)		
Savings account	_____	_____
401K	_____	_____
IRA	_____	_____
Other	_____	_____
Total Savings:	_____	_____
Housing		
Mortgage/rent	_____	_____
Insurance	_____	_____
Property taxes	_____	_____

Expense Category	Amount Paid Last Month	Usual Monthly Cost
Electricity	_____	_____
Heating	_____	_____
Water	_____	_____
Sanitation	_____	_____
Telephone	_____	_____
Cleaning	_____	_____
Repairs	_____	_____
Maintenance	_____	_____
Supplies	_____	_____
Other	_____	_____
Total Housing:	_____	_____
Total Food:	_____	_____
(Groceries only)		

Clothing

	Amount Paid Last Month	Usual Monthly Cost
His	_____	_____
Hers	_____	_____
Children's	_____	_____
Accessories	_____	_____
Other	_____	_____
Total Clothing:	_____	_____

Transportation

	Amount Paid Last Month	Usual Monthly Cost
Insurance	_____	_____
Gas	_____	_____
Oil	_____	_____
Repairs	_____	_____
Maintenance	_____	_____
Parking	_____	_____
Other	_____	_____
Total Transportation:	_____	_____

Expense Category	Amount Paid Last Month	Usual Monthly Cost
Entertainment		
Recreation	_____	_____
Dining out	_____	_____
Movies	_____	_____
Concerts	_____	_____
Baby sitters	_____	_____
Magazines	_____	_____
Newspapers	_____	_____
Vacation	_____	_____
Clubs	_____	_____
Activities	_____	_____
Other	_____	_____
Total Entertainment:	_____	_____
Medical		
Insurance	_____	_____
Doctors	_____	_____
Dentists	_____	_____
Medication	_____	_____
Total Medical:	_____	_____
Insurance		
Life	_____	_____
Disability	_____	_____
Other	_____	_____
Total Insurance:	_____	_____
Children		
School lunches	_____	_____
Allowances	_____	_____
Tuition	_____	_____
Lessons	_____	_____

Expense Category	Amount Paid Last Month	Usual Monthly Cost
Child-care		
Other		
Total Children:		

Gifts

Christmas		
Birthdays		
Anniversaries		
Other		
Total Gifts:		

Miscellaneous

Toiletries		
Husband misc.		
Wife misc.		
Children misc.		
Dry cleaning		
Laundry		
Animal care		
Hair care		
Other		
Total Miscellaneous:		

Total Expenses:		

Net Worth

The one financial statement that summarizes every financial transaction that a couple has ever made is the net worth statement. A net worth statement is a picture at a particular point in time of the true financial position of a family. This statement shows the assets a family owns and the total debts or liabilities it owes.

Subtracting the liabilities from the assets gives the net worth.

If you measure your net worth periodically, you'll be able to see whether or not you are making progress toward your financial goals.

Assets

Liquid (convertible into cash within seven days)

Cash on hand and checking account balance $ _____

Money market funds   _____

CDs (interest rate _____%)   _____

Savings (interest rate _____%)   _____

Life insurance cash values   _____

Other: _____   _____

Total Liquid Assets: $_____

(Transfer the total to the Personal Balance Sheet Analysis on page 144.)

Nonliquid (cannot be sold quickly except at a loss)

Home (market value) $ _____

Land (market value)   _____

Business valuation   _____

Real estate investments   _____

Limited partnerships   _____

Boat, camper, tractor, etc.   _____

Automobile(s) (market value)   _____

Furniture and personal property (market value)   _____

Coin and stamp collections, antiques   _____

IRAs and Keogh   _____

Pension and profit-sharing   _____

Receivables from others   _____

Other: _____   _____

Total Nonliquid Assets: $ _____

(Transfer the total to the Personal
Balance Sheet Analysis.)

Liabilities

	Creditor	Interest Rate	Balance Due
1.	$ _____	_____	_____
2.	_____	_____	_____
3.	_____	_____	_____
4.	_____	_____	_____
5.	_____	_____	_____
6.	_____	_____	_____
7.	_____	_____	_____
8.	_____	_____	_____
9.	_____	_____	_____
10.	_____	_____	_____
Total Liabilities:	$ _____	_____	_____

(Transfer the total to the Personal
Balance Sheet Analysis.)

Personal Balance Sheet Analysis

(Date: _____)

Liquid assets	$	_____
Plus nonliquid assets	+	_____
Total Assets	=	_____
Less Total Liabilities	–	_____
Net Worth	=	_____